The Reaching Hand
of Self-Defiance

Dey Ten

BookLeaf Publishing
India | USA | UK

Presentation by *BookLeaf Publishing*

Web: www.bookleafpub.com

E-mail: info@bookleafpub.com

ISBN: 9789357448260

First edition 2021

PREFACE

How do we define ourselves? How free are we
in our decisions?
These questions and others I ask myself, not
always finding answers. This collection is the
result of questioning this things, and dreaming
of others.

Leaves

The fall of leaves - hypnotic
twirling For those who dream of
happy ends, The nature's sleep this
year is early It can't escape time's
shifting sands

Yet what we see is just the beauty
And wonder, why is it so sad?
It's more than that - it knows its duty,
To go the way it always had.

It leads with hope -
And we shall follow,
It goes ahead -
And we shall see.

No soul is empty,
No mind -
hollow,

As long as it still tries to be.

Beginning

Oh, the beginning!
Few feeble feelings flowing
Through thoughts that try to take
Them all
And see if it results in growing
Of own being
Or own goal
And when they see at last
A thought will feel
First time in its existence
At least for once
And understand what's real
And what is not.
Then it will cease resistance
Against its own world.
The freedom of the
mind Brings something
new More than just
living Reality just grew
Few feeble feelings now decide,
What will be said?
Oh, the beginning,
Or the end?

Create.

Create my friend,
Indifference kills passion
In such a way
That it remains alive, and yet
There   is   no   more
progression No motivation
to be held
At least today
At least for now
No place to lay your truth upon the others
The voices will say
There is no truce for losers
And you'll drown
And still survive
Still reaching out your hand
Still being drawn
To life
To finding new land
Just don't forget to
wait
Just don't give up, my friend,
Create.

The Battle

The mind is
trapped Unable to
escape Inside own
wishes To create
To finally be free
To finally be great
Or possibly just be.
It's filled with anger, vicious
justice With hateful hope and
fading grace It may be righteous
Or maybe a disgrace
In any case, an endless battle
The worst kind to be fought
Against the self
It's always fatal
The victim of own thought
It tries just to exist
For greatness to see
Or being good at
least Or possibly just
be.

Post poetry

To stay updated is no easy task
The flow of time is rich in information
The age of now is still choosing a mask
From all the masks of cultural creation

Postmodern thoughts ironically grew
old Post-irony has out-post its brothers
And just as meta-modernism told:
"We're all equal, just some more than the
others."

Post-time:
post-measures May each
join its chorus To sing
along:
O tempora, o mores.

Mountains

A snowy path of magnificent
grace And falling flakes
All leading clear, but unsuspecting gaze
To frozen lakes
To glossy ice, reflecting landscapes
That reach the sky and clouds
Without any sounds
With just a peaceful silence
With nobody around
At all
Earth's greatest creations
Yet all they know
Is standing there untroubled
That's all they need
In an eternal show
Just touched by time, a little crumbled
And covered in snow.

Last one

The one who drops the ball
Has to pick it up,
Or their immortal
soul Without any luck
Will willfully create the consequences
To indicate who is
And who is not themselves,
The real difference between the two is
understanding
Pick up the ball
To find yourself created
By your own hand
Become the last one standing.

Human

What does it mean to fight
With disregard of reason
But being just a human?
Like nature every season
An endless change of turning
Of each state.
What difference does it make?
Creating our own justice
For own sake
We fight against
ourselves Because we
want
Through our fight we're proven
And it results in nothing
But being a just human.

Patterns

It's wonderful to see how patterns are created
From almost nothing but some basic rules
In life and universe nothing is just wasted
And everything is following same ques

And we, a drop of life in darkness
Are looking outwards
Does universe define us?
Like it defines our lands?

The question remains,
Do we decide?
Are we holding the
reins Of our lives?

Soul

A real soul does never
sleep It's transient like
water
It flows from one
dream To another
Without drawing a line
Or seeing any difference
Or having to decline
Decisions are unreal
It finds its truth in solace
Of being just as real -
A real soul dreams always.

The Greates Achievement

Creation of the mind
The greatest
achievement To put
yourself aside
From what the world has given
Yet use it to create
For something more than living
Before it is too late
Before the others see it
Creation of the mind
How great it is
How living.

Silence

Let's take a walk without even moving
Yet come so far that we get lost
In the unknown (it's oddly soothing)
Where anyone appears to be a ghost

We'll see each other as the essence
Of concepts and of thoughts
If wishes and of lessons
That life has taught us both,

We'll dive into ideas
We'll feel each other's souls
We'll share the same ideals
We'll choose our own roles.

And after merely
moments Of speaking our
minds
We find ourselves in silence
And we turn off the lights.

Traveler

A traveler from long forgotten lands
Has come to serve the cause of travel,
To hear the cries, to touch the reaching hands,
To pay the price for what he can't unravel,

And where he goes he sees the need for
help His words of wisdom reach the minds
of all, In empty halls he rings his hollow
bell
His soul remind him of his unpaid toll,

And when he leaves, the silence will follow
No cries to hear, no hands to see,
The words are gone, the minds are hollow
The ringing bell demands it's fee,

He pays his price in never knowing
Whom did he help? Where did he go?
He never left, and yet he's going
Is he a hero or a foe?

A traveler from long forgotten
lands Has come to find the cause of
travel
To stop his cries, to stop his reaching hands

From hiding that what he cannot unravel.

Free

Free thought is not to be controlled
At least not all the time
A lot of what we think we
feel And it is fine.

An uncontrolled thought may lead
To greater purpose
We didn't know we need
It was under the surface
A metamorphic seed
And even if it hurts us
It's making us complete.

Now

The time is now
Which means we go
Towards the broken bridges
Towards the doors without hinges
We go alone
We go on now
It is the only way
At least we go
At least we know
But how? How now?
We never did.
We always felt
And found that out
Today.

Dialogue

"Please promise me, please do remember
That I once was the one who wished for
good And that I didn't lose, nor did surrender
And that I was the only one who understood

Against what force you went into the battle
To keep the oath you made yourself
To seek the worse to make it better
To leave your heaven to fix hell

I didn't lose, nor I surrendered
The flow of time has finally caught up
It made a blow that wasn't ours to handle
The fight of fate itself has given up"

"I promise you, my friend, I won't forget
You stayed with me until the end without regret
You didn't try your best - you gave it all
And now it's time to rest your brave soul

Yet I will fight the fate itself if needed
Because this fight is mine, I need it
Because it's all I have
My cause will be enough.

And even if I lose
I will have you,
My truth."

Voices

No voice that's coming from
inside Is truthfully yourself
The mind is quick to see and hide
Inside its own shell

All masks it has created
Are wearing themselves
Are looking to be
baited And screaming
for help

Don't listen, friend,
Or rather, don't believe
In what they have to
say Believe in what is
real - In what is now,
today.

Choice

A subtle breeze of summer in the evening
Fresh air is bringing back the past
The life feels light and lightly more freeing
It's just a moment, it is not made to last.

A few red rays are piercing cloudy skylines
Are opening the gates to other worlds
A round valley surrounded by the highlands
Small world itself is speaking its own words

Behind the valley and its rocky guardians
Are lying endless fields of wheat
A golden sea of orange
radiance Is moved so gently by
the wind,

And in between the two dimensions
Is standing one to see it all
To feel the wind, to feel temptation
Of choosing one to gift his soul
Or maybe not to choose at all.

To stay and see the nature's passion
Of shifting times and changing lands
To feel the wind without temptation
To have the freedom without sense

And maybe live, above all else.

Longing

How easily does change
The human kind
To say the least
How individual range
Defined by lust and logic
By wanting to unwind
And sometimes longing
But mostly hate and love
And always hoping
For freedom and for choice,
To just defy the nature
And being locked up by
it Or volunteer for it
Or not being at all.
Without voice
Without right to call
For measures,
To make at least some
noise Is every human being
Deprived of life
And that's the reason
Why even one who's kneeling
Still has the only treasure
Of just being alive
Defined by its
growing

By hate and love
By choice and
hope
And sometimes longing.

Irony

Today it's difficult to not to speak ironic
The irony has conquered all minds
I wouldn't wonder if it becomes iconic
The age of laughter came to claim its rights.

And, to be honest, is anyone to blame?
We didn't choose the circumstance of time
The choice we've got is just to give a name
And since it's irony, it isn't worth a dime.

We laugh at everything around us
Because that's all that we can do
Behind the jokes the truth is ours,
And after all, it's funny 'cause it's
true.

I am.

I am a summary of times
Of shapes and patterns
Truths and lies
Hypocrisy and rules
Of words and letters
In summary - of all things that have happened
And also soon to come.
For worse or maybe
better It all defines,
Yet it's not all what matters,
I'm also what I want
To freely shape with strength and will
With principles and reason
But also love
If nothing's truly
real I hope at least
It will.

www.ingramcontent.com/pod-product-compliance
Lightning Source LLC
LaVergne TN
LVHW050311210726
843507LV00020B/3053